REVELATOR
WORKBOOK

TOMMY MILLER

TWS | THE WRITER'S SOCIETY PUBLISHING

To request permissions, contact TWS Publishing at www.thewriterssociety.online

Paperback: ISBN 978-1-961180-30-7

TWS Publishing
Lodi, CA
www.thewriterssociety.online

CONTENTS

CHAPTER 1
CREATING PROPHETIC
COMMUNITIES

INTRODUCTION:

Chapter One serves as a foundational guide in the journey of
building prophetic communities and embracing our true identity
in Christ. This chapter explores the dynamics of revelatory spiritual gifts, the transformative power of understanding our true
identity, and the essential principles of perceiving others through a
spiritual lens. As we delve into the material, we will uncover key
insights shaping our perspective on spiritual gifts, human identity,
and the profound connection between humanity and Divinity.

The following workbook questions are designed to deepen your
understanding of the concepts presented in Chapter One, encouraging reflection and application in the context of cultivating a
prophetic culture. Let's embark on this exploration together,
seeking to align our perceptions with the truth revealed in the

Scriptures and laying the groundwork for a transformative journey toward prophetic living.

WORKBOOK QUESTIONS

1. Understanding Revelatory Spiritual Gifts

According to the text, why are revelatory spiritual gifts, not something to strive for but rather a natural occurrence in our lives?

What is the key to activating spiritual gifts in our everyday natural environment?

How did Jesus operate in revelatory giftings, and what can we learn from His example?

Why is it crucial to establish a correct perception, and how does it relate to creating a prophetic culture?

2. Embracing Our True Identity

Summarize the significance of Second Corinthians 5:14-17 in understanding our true identity in Christ.

Define "hamartia" and explain how it relates to being out of sync with our true identity.

How does the inclusion of all humanity in the death,

burial, and resurrection of Jesus transform our perception of others?

Why is it essential to move from evaluating others based on their external appearances to recognizing their spiritual identity?

3. Humanity's Transformation in Christ

Explain the concept of "old things have passed away; behold, all things have become new" in the context of our identity in Christ.

How does understanding humanity's inclusion in the Incarnation of Jesus contribute to building a prophetic community?

In what ways can focusing solely on external behaviors miss the essence of a prophetic culture?

What is our role as a prophetic culture according to the text

4. Transcending Earthly Labels

What does the phrase "Even though we have known Christ according to the flesh, yet now we know Him thus no longer" signify?

Explain the shift from astonishment to offense in the context of viewing others through earthly, fleshly identities.

Provide an example from the text illustrating the consequences of viewing Jesus through earthly relationships.

How does Jesus' approach to John the Baptist demonstrate perceiving someone through the Spirit rather than the flesh?

5. Embracing Humanity's Divine Identity

What is the responsibility of individuals in a prophetic culture when encountering others?

How does perceiving others in the heavenly realms contribute to prophesying into their future and true identity?

Explain the connection between acknowledging, uplifting, encouraging others, and recognizing their divine essence.

According to Matthew 10:40, what is the profound connection between humanity and Divinity?

6. Embracing Our Resurrected Identity

How does John's Gospel differ from other gospel accounts in presenting Jesus' lineage?

What is the significance of the statement "In the beginning was the Word, and the Word was with God, and the Word was God"?

How does recognizing our true origin in Christ impact our understanding of human lineage?

Why is perceiving one another as the resurrected bride of Christ crucial in cultivating prophetic cultures?

CLOSING REFLECTIONS:

As we conclude our exploration of Chapter One, "Creating Prophetic Communities," we have navigated through the profound principles of revelatory spiritual gifts, the transformative nature of our true identity in Christ, and the importance of perceiving others through a spiritual lens. The insights shared in this chapter invite us to a paradigm shift in our understanding of spiritual gifts, relationships, and the inherent divinity within each individual.

May these workbook questions be catalysts for personal reflection, group discussions, and practical application in your journey toward building a prophetic culture. As you engage with the material, consider how these truths can shape your interactions within your community, family, and beyond. Embracing the revelation of our divine identity and recognizing others in their true spiritual essence lays the groundwork for a powerful prophetic community.

. . .

Let the principles discussed in this chapter resonate in your heart, guiding you as you seek to live out a prophetic life and foster a culture of honor, understanding, and engagement with the spiritual gifts bestowed upon us.

In the following chapters, we will delve deeper into the nuances of prophetic living, building upon the foundation laid in Chapter One. May your journey be transformative and may the prophetic culture you cultivate bring glory to God and blessing to those around you.

ADDITIONAL QUESTIONS:

Activation of Spiritual Gifts:

- In your experience, have you ever witnessed or experienced the activation of revelatory spiritual gifts in a way that aligns with the principles discussed in the chapter?
- Share the details of the experience and how it impacted your perception of spiritual gifts.

Overcoming Earthly Labels:

- Reflect on a time when you may have unintentionally viewed someone through their earthly identity or external appearance.
- How did this impact your interactions with them, and what lessons can be drawn from this experience in the

context of building a prophetic culture that transcends earthly labels?

Application in Community Life:

- Consider your local church community or another community you are a part of.
- How might the principles of perceiving others through a spiritual lens and embracing humanity's divine identity contribute to fostering a culture of honor, understanding, and engagement with spiritual gifts within that community?
- Share practical steps or ideas for implementing these principles.

CHAPTER 2
OUT WITH THE OLD — IN WITH THE NEW

INTRODUCTION

In the labyrinth of theological exploration, the realms of prophecy beckon us to unravel the intricacies between the Old and New Testaments. Chapter two takes us on a transformative journey, peeling back layers to discern the essence of prophecy in the context of divine dispensations. As we delve into the heart of discernment, the revelator unveils the distinctiveness between the prophetic gifts of yesteryears and the vibrant tapestry of the New Covenant.

This exploration is not merely an academic pursuit but a roadmap for cultivating a pure expression of the prophetic within the contemporary local church. Guided by the author's teachings, we navigate the landscape of "prophetic dispensation," seeking to shield the New Testament prophetic gift from the shadows of Old

Covenant practices. At its core, this revelation urges us to embrace a prophetic paradigm that aligns with the edification, exhortation, and comfort intended by the divine design.

Join us as we journey through the chapters, dissecting the wisdom imparted by the author, unraveling the significance of John the Baptist's unique role, and peering into the language of Heaven that shapes the New Testament prophetic narrative. Along the way, we'll encounter the concept of "foretelling," explore the prophetic responsibility bestowed upon believers, and contemplate the obsolete nature of the Old Testament prophetic office.

In the echo of each page, let the words resonate — a call to transcend theological boundaries and grasp the dynamic, life-altering implications of understanding prophecy in the light of the New Covenant. Welcome to a space where ancient truths meet contemporary revelations, forging a path "out with the old—in with the new."

WORKBOOK QUESTIONS

1. Understanding the Distinction:

Why is it crucial to discern the distinction between the Old Testament and New Testament gift and office of prophecy?

What are the potential consequences of misapplying Old Covenant principles to New Testament prophecy?

2. Prophetic Dispensation:

Explain the concept of "prophetic dispensation" and its significance in preventing the New Testament prophetic gift from mimicking Old Testament ways.

What paradigm shift occurred with the arrival of Jesus in terms of the prophetic office, and why is it essential to align the prophetic gift with its intended function in the local church?

3. Three Dispensations in Matthew 11:

Identify and describe the three distinct dispensations outlined in Matthew 11 regarding prophetic ministry.

How does the role of John the Baptist mark a transition from the Old Testament prophetic era to the New Covenant prophetic era?

4. Role of John the Baptist:

Explain the significance of John the Baptist's role in announcing the Messiah's arrival.

How does John the Baptist's proclamation differentiate

from the focus of Old Testament prophets, and what does it signify for the New Covenant believers?

5. New Testament Prophetic Guidance:

Summarize the guidance provided in 2 Peter 1:16-19 for seeking illumination, strategy, or guidance in the New Testament.

Contrast the role and function of prophets in the Old Testament with the principles governing New Testament prophecy, as highlighted in the passage.

6. Foretelling in New Testament Prophecy:

Define "foretelling" as an aspect of New Testament prophetic gifting.

Provide examples from Acts 11 and Paul's journey to illustrate how foretelling prophecies in the New Testament differ from Old Testament prophecies.

7. The Language of Heaven:

According to Hebrews 1:1-2, how did God communicate with the fathers in the past, and how does He communicate with believers in the present?

Explain the concept of the prophetic word originating from Christ and its connection to the language of Heaven.

8. Application and Implications:

How does understanding the distinction between New Testament and Old Testament prophecy have real-life consequences?

Reflect on a situation where the principles of New Testament prophecy (edification, exhortation, and comfort) could have positively impacted someone's life.

9. Prophetic Responsibility:

Summarize the prophet's responsibility as outlined in the concluding statements of the material.

In what ways can the prophetic office and gift of the Old Testament be considered obsolete, and what is the new purpose introduced in the New Covenant?

10. Personal Reflection:

Consider your own beliefs about prophecy and its role in the church.

How does the material presented challenge or align with your current understanding?

CLOSING REFLECTIONS:

As we draw the curtain on exploring chapter two we find ourselves standing at the crossroads of ancient wisdom and contemporary revelation. The journey through the distinct dispensations of prophecy, the prophetic role of John the Baptist, and the language of Heaven has been a quest for clarity in a realm often shrouded in ambiguity.

In the wake of this revelatory odyssey, let the resounding truth echo in our hearts: the prophetic landscape has shifted. With its judgments and foreboding, the Old Covenant's prophetic office has faded into the annals of history. In its place, the New Covenant offers a vibrant tapestry where prophecy is a symphony of edification, exhortation, and comfort.

As we navigate our lives and communities, armed with the understanding of these divine shifts, let us be torchbearers of the New Testament prophetic—anointed not with suspicion and doom but with the radiant light of Christ's finished work. Our prophetic responsibility is not to foretell impending judgment but to declare, "It is finished," aligning ourselves with the language of Heaven.

May the echoes of this revelation ripple through our understanding, transforming how we perceive and practice prophecy within the tapestry of the local church. In bidding farewell to the old, we usher in a new era—a prophetic era inter-twined with grace, unity, and the harmonious interdependence of believers.

As we step out of these pages and back into our lives, may the truths uncovered here empower us to be conduits of the New Covenant prophetic — a beacon of hope, encouragement, and comfort in a world hungering for the authenticity of divine revelation. In the grand narrative of God's unfolding plan, let our prophetic voices resound with the eternal truth — out with the old, in with the new.

ADDITIONAL QUESTIONS:

Prophetic Alignment:

- How can recognizing the distinction between the Old and New Testament prophetic gifts contribute to aligning the prophetic gift within the local church?
- In what ways might misunderstanding this distinction lead to a misapplication of the prophetic gift, and what impact could it have on individuals and the community?

John the Baptist's Significance:

- Explore the unique role of John the Baptist as outlined in Matthew 11.

- How does his proclamation mark a shift in the prophetic era, and what implications does it hold for the New Covenant believers?
- Reflect on the idea that even the least in the kingdom of heaven surpasses John the Baptist in the New Testament prophetic era.
- What does this mean for the role and stature of believers in the prophetic?

Foretelling vs. Predicting:

- Distinguish between the concept of "foretelling" in New Testament prophecy and the idea of predicting future events.
- How does the foretelling aspect align with the principles of edification, exhortation, and comfort?
- Can you think of modern-day scenarios where a foretelling prophetic message could provide guidance without instilling fear or judgment?
- How does this differ from Old Testament predictive prophecies?

PRACTICAL APPLICATION:

- Reflect on the statement that New Testament prophecy is rooted in relationships, community, and unity.

- How can these elements be practically incorporated into the operation of the prophetic gift within a local church setting?
- Share examples or personal experiences where the New Testament prophetic approach of edification, exhortation, and comfort has positively impacted individuals or a community.

LANGUAGE OF HEAVEN IN PRACTICE:

- Explore the concept that the prophetic word originates from Christ and is rooted in His finished work.
- How does this understanding influence the way believers approach prophesying healing, restoration, or other manifestations?
- Consider a practical scenario where aligning with the language of Heaven, rooted in Christ's reality, could bring about a transformative prophetic encounter.
- How does this differ from an Old Testament prophetic approach?

CHAPTER 3
IN PROPORTION TO OUR FAITH

INTRODUCTION:

Welcome to Chapter Three, "In Proportion to Our Faith," where we embark on a journey through the transformative landscape of spiritual gifts and prophetic revelations in the New Testament. In this chapter, we witness a distinct shift from the roles of Old Testament prophets to the dynamic realm of New Testament prophecy. The focus moves from waiting for divine directives to a profound emphasis on faith and the believer's authority in the prophetic. Join us as we explore the insights offered by the Apostle Paul in Romans 12, unraveling the intricacies of the gift of prophecy and its connection to faith.

The exploration delves into the essence of faith — far beyond a mere internal strength but as an alternative perspective, aligning with the divine blueprint. We'll uncover the pre-written perspective of faith, making the invisible visible, and the realization that every believer possesses a gift of faith that cannot be increased or diminished. Additionally, we confront the obstacles to faith, discovering that sight, rather than the devil, can be the adversary.

As we journey through the principles outlined in this chapter, we'll grasp the interplay between spoken words, corresponding actions, and the tangible manifestation of prophetic beliefs. The teachings highlight the transformative power of faith in God's perspective, offering a lens through which we can shape reality according to heaven's design.

Join us as we explore the depths of faith, prophecy, and the practical application of revelatory gifts in the New Testament context, seeking not just understanding but a transformation of our own perspectives and actions.

WORKBOOK QUESTIONS:

1. Understanding New Testament Prophecy:

What is the key distinction between Old Testament prophets and New Testament revelatory gifts?

How does the focus shift from the Old Testament to the New Testament concerning prophecy?

2. Romans 12 and the Gift of Prophecy:

According to Romans 12:6, how should individuals with the gift of prophecy use it?

Explain the concept of "prophesying in proportion to our faith" as mentioned in Romans 12:6.

3. The Role of Faith in Prophecy:

How does the gift of prophecy in the New Testament differ from Old Testament prophecy?

What is the significance of faith in the exercise of prophetic and revelatory gifts?

4. Faith as an Alternative Perspective:

According to the text, what is the nature of faith? How does it differ from common misconceptions?

How does maintaining a single-minded perspective contribute to clarity and peace?

5. Faith and the Invisible Perspective:

Contrast the concept of speaking something into existence with the true essence of prophecy.

Explain how faith transforms the unseen into the visible, drawing from Hebrews 11:1.

6. The Gift of Faith:

How is faith described as a gift in the text?
Can it be increased or diminished according to the author?

Discuss the importance of aligning with the gift of faith and avoiding alternative perspectives.

7. Overcoming Obstacles to Faith:

Who or what is identified as the obstacle to faith in the text? Explain the role of sight in hindering faith.

How can one overcome obstacles to faith according to the teachings in James 1:6?

8. Faith Requires Action:

Provide examples from the text that illustrate the connection between spoken words and corresponding actions.

Why is it emphasized that faith requires corresponding actions?

How does this relate to true belief?

9. Application of Prophetic Ability:

Discuss the practical aspects of prophesying over challenging situations as mentioned in the text.

How can individuals apply prophetic and revelatory gifts to shape reality according to heaven's design?

SUMMARY AND REFLECTION:

- Summarize the key points regarding faith, prophecy, and the exercise of revelatory gifts in the New Testament.
- Reflect on how these teachings can be applied in your own life and spiritual journey.

CONCLUDING REFLECTIONS:

As we conclude our exploration of Chapter Three, "In Proportion to Our Faith," may these insights into the dynamics of New Testament prophecy and the profound connection to faith leave a lasting imprint on your spiritual journey. The teachings from Romans 12 have unveiled a shift from the Old Testament prophetic era to a New Testament landscape where believers are empowered to prophesy in alignment with their faith.

Let the understanding that faith is not a variable, but a perspective guide you beyond the rudimentary aspects of belief in God. Embrace the gift of faith and its transformative power, aligning with God's perspective as the pinnacle of sonship.

· · ·

As you navigate the intricacies of faith and prophecy, remember the crucial interplay between spoken words and corresponding actions. Let your faith be demonstrated through tangible expressions, echoing the profound truth that faith requires action.

May this chapter serve as a roadmap, leading you to a deeper understanding of faith's pre-written perspective and the transformative potential of prophetic and revelatory gifts. As you apply these principles in your life, may you experience the undeniable force of faith in shaping reality according to heaven's design.

In the journey ahead, may your faith be unwavering, your words carry the essence of heaven, and your actions be a testament to the transformative power of faith in God's perspective. Until we embark on the next chapter, may you walk boldly in the light of faith, shaping your reality in accordance with the divine blueprint.

CHAPTER 4

EXPRESSING GIFTS THROUGH IDENTITY

INTRODUCTION:

Welcome to the captivating journey into the realm of spiritual gifts as we explore the profound insights laid out in Chapter Four: "Expressing Gifts Through Identity." In this enlightening chapter, we delve into the timeless words of the Apostle Paul in 1 Corinthians 12, where he unveils the fascinating diversity of the gifts of the Spirit. Through verses 4-10, Paul intricately guides us through the essence of these divine endowments, reminding us that these gifts are not merely individual talents but a collective manifestation of the same Spirit, the same Lord, and the same God working for the benefit of all.

In the pages that follow, we embark on a captivating journey through the gifts of wisdom, knowledge, prophecy, and discernment, discovering how these gifts find their expression in the authentic identity of believers. Drawing inspiration from the Mirror Bible, we unravel the truth that every expression of the Spirit serves to bring into focus the profound work accomplished in Christ. As we navigate through the examples of Jesus, the ultimate revealer of divine truth, we witness how these gifts seamlessly operate as an unstrained outpouring of one's authentic self.

Join us as we uncover the wisdom that guides our actions, the knowledge that reveals hidden truths, the prophetic voice that echoes divine messages, and the discernment that navigates unseen spiritual realities. This chapter invites us to explore these gifts not as isolated phenomena but as an integral part of our identity as beloved sons and daughters of God.

So, let the pages turn, and the journey unfold as we delve into the mysteries of spiritual gifts, understanding that their expression is not confined to sacred spaces but is meant to naturally emanate from the core of who we are.

WORKBOOK QUESTIONS:

1. Understanding Gifts of the Spirit

What are the three categories of spiritual gifts mentioned in 1 Corinthians 12:4-10?

How does the Mirror Bible describe the purpose of the manifestation of the Spirit in each individual?

In what way does the chapter suggest that expressing the gifts of the Spirit is tied to revealing what God has accomplished in Christ?

2. Word of Wisdom

Define the Thayer Greek Lexicon's definition of wisdom.

How does the word of wisdom differ from general or human wisdom?

Provide an example from the chapter (using John 21:4-7) that illustrates Jesus operating in the word of wisdom.

3. Word of Knowledge

Distinguish between the word of knowledge and prophecy as explained in the chapter.

What characterizes the word of knowledge, and how does it differ from regular human knowledge?

Explain the encounter between Jesus and the woman at the well as an example of the word of knowledge.

4. Prophecy

Define prophecy as explained in the chapter.

How does New Testament prophecy, as discussed in the chapter, differ from Old Testament prophecy regarding famines?

Provide an example of a New Testament prophecy mentioned in the chapter and its purpose.

5. Discerning of Spirits

Define the gift of discerning of spirits according to the chapter.

How did Jesus use the gift of discerning of spirits in the example given in Mark 2:8?

In what ways does the chapter emphasize the importance of discernment in navigating spiritual realms?

6. Natural Expression of Gifts

How does the chapter emphasize Jesus's natural expression of revelatory gifts without using religious terminology?

Explain why the chapter suggests that expressing revelatory gifts should be a natural outpouring of one's authentic identity.

According to the chapter, how can individuals tap into their prophetic gifts more frequently in everyday life?

7. Embracing Revelatory Gifts

According to Paul's conclusion in 1 Corinthians 12, what does he urge believers to prioritize?

How does the Mirror Bible express the idea of pursuing the highest good in the context of spiritual gifts?

Summarize the chapter's message on wholeheartedly embracing one's identity as a revelator and expressing spiritual gifts in the pursuit of love.

CLOSING REFLECTIONS:

As we conclude this insightful exploration of Chapter Four, "Expressing Gifts Through Identity," we find ourselves standing on the threshold of a profound truth – that spiritual gifts are not distant, mystical occurrences but an inherent part of our identity as believers. Paul's guidance in 1 Corinthians 12 calls us to embrace the diversity of these gifts, recognizing that each one is a unique expression of the same divine Spirit.

In our journey through the word of wisdom, the word of knowledge, prophecy, and the discerning of spirits, we've witnessed how these gifts, when authentically expressed, become a natural outpouring of our divine nature. The Mirror Bible beautifully reminds us that as we eagerly explore our favorite gifts, we should also be introduced to the *"summum bonum"* of life – the highest good. As the chapter conveys, this highest good is found in the pursuit of love, reflecting the heart of God.

So, let us wholeheartedly embrace our identity as revelators, allowing these gifts to flow naturally and effortlessly in our lives. Whether in mundane conversations or significant life decisions, may wisdom, knowledge, prophecy, and discernment spring forth as an extension of our authentic selves. As we passionately pursue love, let these gifts serve as tangible evidence of the divine presence in our lives.

May the mysteries of spiritual gifts continue to unfold, inspiring us to tap into our prophetic nature more frequently, not confined to specific settings but seamlessly integrated into the fabric of our daily existence. In pursuing love and expressing these gifts, we discover a transformative power that transcends the ordinary, aligning us with the divine purpose woven into the very core of our being.

With these reflections, we bid farewell to Chapter Four, carrying with us the profound truth that expressing our spiritual gifts is not just a calling but an authentic revelation of our identity as beloved children of God. As we turn the page to the next chapter, let our hearts be open to the continued exploration of the wonders that unfold when we fully embrace the gifts bestowed upon us.

CHAPTER 5
NEW LANGUAGE FOR A NEW CREATION

INTRODUCTION:

As we delve into Chapter Five, "New Language For a New Creation," we explore the intricate topic of the gift of tongues. This subject often stirs debate, particularly among those new to the church, as questions arise about its relevance, proper functioning, and where it fits within the broader context of scripture. In this chapter, we will dissect the complexities surrounding the gift of tongues, examining the Western versus Eastern interpretations, the limited mentions of tongues in scripture, the practical aspects of how it works, and the three distinct functions it serves.

WORKBOOK QUESTIONS:

1. Understanding Western vs. Eastern Interpretation

Why do you think the Western church tends to create

fixed doctrines around biblical concepts, while the Eastern philosophy allows for the coexistence of various truths?

In what ways can adopting an Eastern interpretation mindset impact the understanding of the gift of tongues?

2. Tongues in Scripture

According to Mark 16:17-18, what signs did Jesus mention that would follow believers?

How does speaking in new tongues distinguish believers from unbelievers?

Explain the significance of the "law of first mention" principle in interpreting scripture, especially in the context of the gift of tongues.

3. How Tongues Works

Contrast the misconception of speaking in tongues as uncontrollable babbling with the biblical understanding presented in the chapter.

What is the role of the inner ear in the process of speaking in tongues, according to the chapter?

4. Three Functions of Tongues

Describe the first function of speaking in tongues as

evidence to an unbeliever, as demonstrated in Acts 2:1-13.

Why was it considered a supernatural event?

How does Paul address the Corinthians' misuse of spiritual gifts, specifically the gift of tongues, in 1 Corinthians 12 and 14?

5. Revelatory Gifts

List some of the revelatory gifts mentioned in 1 Corinthians 12:4-11.

Why does Paul emphasize that all these gifts serve the same purpose?

Explain the imbalance in the Corinthian church's approach to spiritual gifts, particularly the overemphasis on tongues and the undervaluation of prophecy.

APPLICATION AND REFLECTION:

- Reflect on your own understanding of the gift of tongues before and after reading this chapter.
- Has your perspective changed? If so, how?
- How can the three manifestations of tongues (as a sign, in a group setting with interpretation, for personal edification) be practically applied in the modern-day church context?

CRITICAL THINKING

- Consider the challenges posed by the limited mention of the gift of tongues in scripture.
- How does this impact the formation of doctrines, and how can believers responsibly approach this topic?

PERSONAL EXPERIENCE

- If you have experienced speaking in tongues, share your thoughts on how this practice aligns with the biblical principles discussed in the chapter.
- If you haven't spoken in tongues, how has your understanding of this gift evolved based on the information provided in the chapter?

CLOSING REFLECTIONS:

As we conclude this exploration of Chapter Five, may these questions guide you in deepening your understanding of the gift of tongues and its multifaceted nature. In navigating the Western and Eastern interpretations, examining biblical mentions, and understanding the practical aspects, may you find clarity and wisdom. Let the three functions of tongues illuminate the richness of this gift in diverse contexts, and may your reflections contribute to a more nuanced and informed perspective on this topic within the broader tapestry of spiritual experiences.

CHAPTER 6

GOD'S LINES OF COMMUNICATION

INTRODUCTION:

Welcome to Chapter Six of our exploration into the realms of divine communication — "God's Lines of Communication." In this chapter, we dive into how God speaks to His people and the unique prophetic gifts individuals possess. The journey unfolds through personal experiences, biblical examples, and a deeper understanding of the various modes of communication, ranging from visions and dreams to trances and direct voices.

As we venture into this chapter, consider your encounters with God and how you've sought His voice. Perhaps you've felt isolated, wondering why God seems to speak more intimately to others. Through the narrative and teachings, we aim to demystify the prophetic and bring it closer to home, allowing you to feel at ease in listening to the revelatory voice of God.

Join us as we explore the distinct prophetic gifts of seers, hearers, and knowers, drawing inspiration from biblical passages illustrating how God tailors His communication to the individual. Delve into the significance of impressions, visions, dreams, and trances as unique channels through which God imparts His messages. Discover the importance of interpreting these prophetic messages and their role in shaping our understanding and actions.

Finally, we'll reflect on the pursuit of God's direct voice and the impact of our relationship with Him on interpreting His messages. By the end of this chapter, we hope you'll gain insights into God's diverse lines of communication and find practical ways to cultivate a more intimate and revelatory relationship with the Divine. So, let's embark on this exploration together and unlock the mysteries of God's communication channels.

WORKBOOK QUESTIONS:

1. Reflection on Personal Experience:

Have you ever felt a sense of inadequacy or isolation in your spiritual journey because you perceived others as having a more direct line of communication with God?

Describe your experience.

2. Identifying Prophetic Gifts:

Reflect on the three main ways people receive revelations: seeing, hearing, and knowing.

Which of these modes do you feel most connected to?

Why?

3. Biblical Exploration:

Explore Amos 7:8 and the interaction between God and Amos regarding the plumb line.

How does this passage illustrate the personalized communication style God uses with individuals based on their prophetic gifts?

4. Self-Discovery in Prophetic Circles:

If you were to categorize yourself as a seer, hearer, or knower, which one resonates with you the most?

How do you think recognizing and embracing your prophetic gift can enhance your relationship with God?

5. Impressions as a Mode of Communication:

Consider the concept of impressions in prophetic communication.

Have you ever experienced a strong sense of knowing or a vivid image that felt like it was directly placed in your mind by God?

Share your experience.

6. Interpreting Prophetic Messages:

Reflect on the importance of interpreting prophetic messages, as the text mentions.

Can you recall a time when you received a revelation, and the interpretation significantly impacted your understanding and subsequent actions?

7. Exploring Visions:

Dig into the examples of visions in Acts 9:11-12 and Acts 16:9.

How did these visions guide the individuals involved in their respective situations?

What role did visions play in shaping the early church's trajectory?

8. Significance of Dreams:

Explore the significance of dreams in prophetic communication, referencing the example of Joseph in Genesis 37.

How did Joseph handle his prophetic dream, and what lessons can be drawn from his experience?

9. Understanding Trances:

Consider the explanation of trances and their role in receiving heavenly insights.

Have you ever mistaken a trance for a distraction in your spiritual life?

How might recognizing and embracing trances contribute to a more profound spiritual experience?

10. Personal Perspective on God's Voice:

Reflect on the importance of pursuing the direct voice of God.

Do you feel a desire to hear God's voice in a more audible and direct manner?

How can a balanced perspective on various forms of divine communication enrich your spiritual journey?

11. Impact of Relationship with God:

Explore how your relationship with God shapes your perspective on His messages.

How does your perception of God's love for you influence how you interpret and receive divine communication?

APPLICATION IN DAILY LIFE:

- How can the insights from this chapter be practically applied to your daily life and spiritual journey?
- Consider specific actions or changes in perspective that can enhance your ability to recognize and respond to God's communication.
- Remember to take your time to reflect deeply on these questions and, if possible, discuss them with a mentor, study group, or fellow believers to gain diverse perspectives and insights.

CLOSING REFLECTIONS:

As we conclude our journey through Chapter Six, "God's Lines of Communication," we trust that exploring prophetic gifts, varied communication modes, and biblical examples has brought clarity and encouragement to your spiritual path. Remember that God communicates with His children uniquely and personally, tailored to your individual gifts and experiences.

In your pursuit of understanding God's voice, embrace the diversity of impressions, visions, dreams, and trances as avenues through which divine messages flow. The richness of these experiences is a testament to the multifaceted nature of God's communication.

As you navigate the prophetic realms, cherish your relationship with God, allowing His profound and relentless love to shape your perspective on His messages. Whether you identify as a seer, hearer, knower, or a combination thereof, know that your unique prophetic gift contributes to the beautifully intricate tapestry of the body of Christ.

May the insights gained in this chapter empower you to confidently engage with God's communication channels and foster a deeper connection with the Divine. As you continue your spiritual journey, remain open to the ways in which God chooses to speak to you, and may you find comfort and revelation in His ever-present voice.

CHAPTER 7

THE GIFTS ARE TEMPORARY

INTRODUCTION:

Welcome to this insightful workbook designed to enhance your understanding of the profound concepts explored in Chapter Seven: "The Gifts are Temporary." In this chapter, we delve into the intricate dynamics of spiritual gifts, particularly their purpose, significance, and the interplay between the visible and invisible realms.

As we navigate through the teachings presented in the chapter, we will uncover the essence of prophetic and revelatory gifts, their role in transforming our existence, and the ultimate goal they serve in the grand narrative of spiritual maturity. By examining key passages from 1 Corinthians 13 and Hebrews, we aim to grasp the deeper meanings embedded in the text and draw practical insights for our spiritual journey.

Prepare to explore the delicate balance between the means and the end, understanding the nuanced relationship between spiritual gifts and maturity. This workbook will prompt you to reflect on the profound implications of aligning creation with an untarnished pattern and the authority bestowed upon individuals with revelatory and prophetic gifting.

Engage with the following questions to reinforce your comprehension, provoke thought, and foster a deeper connection with the transformative principles outlined in Chapter Seven. Let the exploration begin!

WORKBOOK QUESTIONS:

1. Understanding the Purpose of Spiritual Gifts:

What is the primary intention of spiritual gifts, according to the discussion in Chapter Seven?

How does Paul challenge the common perception of spiritual gifts in the Western church?

2. Significance of the Word "Perfect":

In verse 10, Paul mentions "when that which is perfect has come." What does the term "perfect" mean in this context?

How does the understanding of the word "perfect" contribute to the overall purpose of spiritual gifts?

3. Role of Prophetic and Revelatory Gifts:

Explain the relationship between prophetic and revelatory gifts and the invisible realm, as discussed in the chapter.

How do these gifts contribute to the transformation of various aspects of existence, according to the text?

4. The Pattern and Authority in Creation:

Elaborate on the concept of drawing from the invisible design and asserting authority over the natural creative world.

How does the use of prophetic and revelatory gifts align with God's creation process, as described in Genesis?

5. Relationship Between Maturity and Spiritual Gifts:

How does Paul emphasize the relationship between maturity and spiritual gifts in the chapter?

Why does Paul assert that spiritual gifts should be set aside as maturity is attained?

6. Purpose of Revelatory Gifts:

According to the text, what is the overarching purpose of revelatory gifts?

How do these gifts contribute to the goal of bringing about a world that mirrors heaven?

7. Application of Revelatory and Prophetic Gifting:

How can a revelatory individual gauge someone's maturity level and speak into their situation?

Provide examples of situations where revelatory and prophetic gifting can be applied to align aspects of life with the Kingdom.

8. Entering God's Rest and Aligning with the Pattern:

Discuss the importance of understanding and pursuing the promise of entering God's rest, as mentioned in Hebrews.

Explain the significance of aligning the visible creation with the pattern that exists apart from it.

9. Creation and the Pattern in Genesis:

Compare the process of God creating light in Genesis with the concept of drawing from the pattern discussed in the chapter.

How does the Word play a crucial role in both the Genesis creation account and the utilization of prophetic authority?

10. The Future of Spiritual Gifts:

According to Paul, why does he predict that spiritual gifts will eventually fade away?

How does the vision of crafting a world mirroring heaven contribute to the understanding of the eventual obsolescence of spiritual gifts?

CLOSING REFLECTIONS:

Congratulations on completing this workbook exploring the profound insights shared in Chapter Seven: "The Gifts are Temporary." By engaging with the questions and reflecting on the teachings, you've embarked on a journey of deeper understanding regarding the purpose and significance of spiritual gifts in the context of your spiritual growth.

As you continue to explore the delicate balance between the visible and invisible realms, may these reflections inspire you to wield your prophetic and revelatory gifts with intentionality, aligning creation with the untarnished pattern from which all things were spoken into existence. Remember, your voice, in partnership with divine intent, holds the power to reshape the fabric of reality and bring about a world that mirrors heaven.

. . .

As you navigate the intricate relationship between maturity and spiritual gifts, may you grow not just as a regulator but as a revelator, bridging the gap between heaven and Earth. Keep in mind the grand vision of crafting a world ruled by individuals bearing the likeness of Jesus, where spiritual gifts serve as catalysts for the manifestation of perfection.

Continue to seek the Alpha and the Omega, drawing from the invisible design and asserting authority over the visible realm. Your journey as a revelatory individual is not just about hearing accurately but about comprehending the heavenly atmosphere and embodying the essence of Jesus in every aspect of your life.

May your exploration of these concepts deepen your spiritual walk, empowering you to bring forth that which is perfect and to usher in the measure of the stature of the fullness of Christ. The journey towards understanding and applying these truths is ongoing, and may you be continually blessed and transformed as you navigate the realms of prophetic and revelatory gifting.

Keep pressing forward on your spiritual journey, and may your revelations align with the divine grace, making a tangible and observable impact on the world around you.

CHAPTER 8

ANTICIPATION

INTRODUCTION:

In the realm of faith and the pursuit of spiritual growth, the concept of anticipation emerges as a powerful force, shaping our outlook on life and influencing the outcomes we experience. Chapter Eight delves into the transformative essence of anticipation, exploring its significance in the context of God's desire to bring forth something entirely new. The narrative unfolds with a call to break free from the limitations of the "next things" mentality and embrace the extraordinary potential inherent in anticipating the new.

As we journey through these pages, we will navigate the intricacies of anticipation within the local church, recognizing its role as a silent yet indispensable core of prophetic ability. The author urges a conscious examination of our expectations, emphasizing the impact of past experiences and the need for a day of repentance—a turning away from the cycle of anticipating only the "next things" in life.

Woven into the fabric of this exploration are five compelling Bible stories, each offering profound insights into the dynamic interplay between expectation and manifestation. From the desperate cries for mercy to the healing touch of a garment's edge, these stories exemplify the nuanced relationship between anticipation and the unfolding of divine encounters.

Amidst the guidance offered, the chapter advocates for a conscious shift in perspective, encouraging readers to set their expectations high and align with the prophetic pull of the future rather than being bound by the shadows of the past. Join us on this enlightening journey as we uncover the potency of anticipation, understanding its pivotal role in shaping our reality and experiencing the boundless grace of God's unfolding plan.

WORKBOOK QUESTIONS:

1. Introduction to Anticipation:

What does the author suggest about the significance of newness in the context of God's desire?

How does the author differentiate between the "next things" and the entirely new manifestations?

2. Anticipation in the Local Church:

According to the author, what role does anticipation play in the local church setting?

Why does the author emphasize the importance of intentional focus and clear intention when entering the house of God?

3. Shifting Perspectives in Church Growth:

Explain the difference between the "next thing" mentality and an anticipation focused on the new.

How does the author suggest breaking free from growth barriers in the context of church growth?

4. The Impact of Past Experiences on Anticipation:

In what ways does the natural mind tend to anticipate based on past experiences?

According to the author, how is the spiritual mind's anticipation different from that of the natural mind?

5. Repentance and Changing Anticipations:

What does the author mean by a "day of repentance" in the context of changing anticipations?

How does clinging to the "next things" impact experiencing the freshness and excitement of the new?

6. Expectation and Self-Fulfilling Prophecies:

How can repetitive cycles and systems become self-fulfilling prophecies in the context of anticipation?

What is the author's advice for actively shaping one's expectations in life?

7. Five Bible Stories:

Choose one of the Bible stories mentioned (Matthew 15:21-23, Luke 8:40-47, Lazarus, Peter in Acts) and explain how the expectations of the individuals involved influenced the outcome.

How do these stories illustrate the power of anticipation in shaping experiences?

8. Conscious Examination of Expectations:

According to the author, why is it crucial to consciously examine and take responsibility for one's expectations?

How does the author suggest breaking free from a negative cycle of anticipating disappointing outcomes?

9. Unity in Anticipation:

How does C.S. Lewis's warning about opinions relate to the concept of anticipation discussed in the chapter?

In what ways can aligning with the kingdom perspective foster unity and agreement in anticipation?

PERSONAL REFLECTION:

- Reflect on your own expectations for the future.
- Are they influenced more by past experiences or a prophetic vision of the future?
- How can you actively shift your anticipations to align with God's intended plan for your life, as suggested by the author?

CLOSING REFLECTIONS:

As we draw the curtains on this exploration of anticipation, may these insights become a guiding light in your spiritual journey. Anticipation, as illuminated in Chapter Eight, is not merely a passive expectation of the future; it is a dynamic force that molds our experiences, transforms our realities, and aligns us with the divine purpose.

In the tapestry of faith, where anticipation and manifestation intertwine, we find the invitation to step into the freshness of the new, unburdened by the constraints of the past. Let the stories shared, the reflections offered, and the call to a day of repentance be catalysts for a profound shift in your expectations.

. . .

As you venture forth, may your anticipation be rooted in the prophetic vision of the future, ushering in unity, agreement, and a shared belief in the promise of a new day. The journey continues beyond these words, and as you actively shape your expectations, may you encounter the remarkable manifestations that come with anticipating the new. May your spiritual walk be marked by a conscious alignment with God's intended plan, and may the kingdom perspective guide your every step into the unfolding chapters of life.

CHAPTER 9

THE LOCAL CHURCH

INTRODUCTION:

Welcome to Chapter Nine of our workbook, where we delve into the profound insights presented in the discussion about "The Local Church." In this chapter, we explore the transformative power of the local church in addressing societal challenges, the importance of internal health for city-wide impact, and the necessity of restoring the integrity of the local church body. As we journey through the text, we will discover key principles for fostering healthy relationships within the church, embracing authenticity, and navigating the dynamics of forgiveness.

The chapter begins by drawing parallels between the growth of the kingdom and a mustard seed, emphasizing the small beginnings that lead to thriving communities. It challenges the conventional methods of city transformation, suggesting that the health of individuals within the local church plays a pivotal role.

We'll explore the significance of Peter's declaration in Matthew 16:13-20, highlighting the foundational role of personal transformation in building a robust local church. The chapter advocates for a perspective that sees each individual through the lens of the Father's design, fostering a culture of honor, impartation, and spiritual discernment.

Additionally, we will examine the concept of agapé love, contrasting it with phileó love, and understand its application in responding to offenses within the church community. The discussion extends to the dangers of comparison and the importance of recognizing our unique identities in Christ.

Finally, we'll delve into the heavenly realm, emphasizing the need to see others as Christ sees them. The chapter concludes by challenging us to continually ask the question, "Who do I believe they are?" — urging us to establish the truth of our confessions about others.

As we embark on this journey through Chapter Nine, let's engage deeply with the teachings, reflect on the questions posed, and consider how these principles can shape our understanding of the local church and our relationships within it.

WORKBOOK QUESTIONS:

1. Understanding the Kingdom Growth

What biblical metaphor does the chapter use to describe the growth of the kingdom?

How does the local church contribute to solving the world's problems, according to the chapter?

2. Transforming Cities Through Internal Health

Why does the chapter argue that the transformation of a city relies on the internal health of the local church?

Explain the idea that the local church and the city it serves should become indistinguishable. What is needed for this alignment to occur?

3. Restoring the Integrity of the Local Church

Summarize the key points of Matthew 16:13-20 and its significance for the local church.

How does the chapter suggest restoring the integrity of the local church body?

4. Seeing Others Through the Lens of the Father's Design

What is the significance of the question, "Who do you say I am?" in the context of relational theology?

How does the chapter propose viewing others through the lens of the Father's design?

5. Embracing Your Authentic Self

According to the chapter, why is there no room for comparison in the body of believers?

How can being surrounded by a community that recognizes your unique identity contribute to staying true to yourself?

6. Forgiveness and Identity in Christ

Explain the connection between forgiveness, identity, and transformation as discussed in the chapter.

How does recognizing one's true identity in Christ relate to the act of forgiveness?

7. Agapé Love vs. Phileó Love

Distinguish between agapé love and phileó love as explained in the chapter.

Provide an example from the Corinthian church that illustrates the application of agapé love.

8. Spiritual Discernment and Seeing Christ in Others

How does the chapter interpret the statement "Upon this rock, I'll build my church" in Matthew 16?

What does the chapter emphasize regarding spiritual discernment in relationships within the church?

9. Comparing Ourselves to Others

According to 2 Corinthians 10:12, why is comparing ourselves to others not wise?

How does the chapter warn against negative self-perceptions rooted in comparison?

10. Heavenly Identity and Interacting with Others

What does Hebrews chapter 12 remind believers about their identity and position?

Why does the chapter stress the importance of recognizing the true identity of others before engaging with them?

CLOSING REFLECTIONS:

As we conclude our exploration of Chapter Nine, "The Local Church," we've encountered profound insights into the transformative role of the local church in individual and societal well-being. The chapter has invited us to reconsider conventional approaches to city transformation, urging us to prioritize internal health and personal growth within the church community.

We've reflected on the significance of Peter's declaration in Matthew 16:13-20, emphasizing the foundational importance of personal transformation in building a robust local church. The call to view each other through the lens of the Father's design has resonated as a powerful principle, fostering a culture of honor, impartation, and spiritual discernment.

The exploration of agapé love versus phileó love has challenged our understanding of responding to offenses within the church, encouraging us to choose a transformative approach marked by patience, kindness, and enduring love.

The warning against the pitfalls of comparison has reminded us of the uniqueness of each individual in the body of believers. Embracing our authentic selves and recognizing the true identities of others has been underscored as essential for a flourishing community.

Finally, the chapter has called us to see others as Christ sees them, urging us to continually ask the question, "Who do I believe they are?" This inquiry prompts us to establish the truth of our confessions about others and align our perspectives with the heavenly realm.

. . .

As we carry these insights forward, let us be intentional in applying these principles within our local church communities. May our relationships be marked by love, understanding, and a deep appreciation for the unique identities each member brings to the body of believers. In doing so, we contribute to the fulfillment of the vision laid out in Matthew 16:18 — a church built upon the revelation of the resurrected Christ.

BONUS CHAPTER - PART ONE

INTRODUCTION:

In the intricate tapestry of the intersection between science and spirituality, the phenomenon of glossolalia, or speaking in tongues, stands as a compelling bridge connecting realms often perceived as distinct. In the exploration of this intriguing topic, Kirby De Lanerolle, the founder of WOW Life Church in Sri Lanka, unfolds a captivating journey. Rooted in Pentecostal and Charismatic contexts, his insights delve into the essence of tongue interpretation, the spiritual dynamics of speaking in tongues, and the transformative power that lies within the indwelling of the Holy Spirit.

As we navigate the chapters of De Lanerolle's teachings, we encounter a multifaceted understanding of glossolalia. From the intricacies of interpreting tongues to the profound impact of fasting on spiritual connectivity, his discourse unravels layers of wisdom gained through years of prayer and contemplation. Furthermore, the exploration extends beyond the spiritual realm, touching on the influence of sound on reality, the significance of breaking patterns through language, and the dynamic relationship between the Spirit within and upon a believer.

Join us on this enlightening journey as we unravel the threads of spirituality and science woven together in the rich fabric of Kirby De Lanerolle's insights. Through a series of profound teachings, he invites us to explore the depths of speaking in tongues, the transformative power of fasting, and the intricate dance between the physical and spiritual realms. As we embark on this exploration, we are encouraged to open our hearts and minds to the possibility of a deeper connection with the divine and a more profound understanding of the mysteries that lie at the core of our faith.

WORKBOOK QUESTIONS:

1. Define Glossolalia and its significance in Pentecostal-Charismatic contexts. How is it related to religious worship?

2. What is the essence of tongue interpretation according to Kirby De Lanerolle?

3. Why does he emphasize the need for a solid foundation, as mentioned in the Bible, for interpretation to take place?

4. According to Kirby De Lanerolle, what are the four different ways in which the interpretation of tongues has manifested in his life?

5. Provide examples or personal experiences for each.

6. Explain the spiritual phenomenon of speaking in tongues as described by Kirby De Lanerolle.

7. How does it edify the inner man, and what is the importance of interpreting this edification?

8. Discuss the importance of the Holy Spirit's indwelling according to Christian theology.

9. How does it set believers apart, and what role does it play in spiritual rebirth?

10. What role does fasting play in the context of speaking in tongues, as suggested by Kirby De Lanerolle?

11. How does fasting weaken the flesh and enhance connectivity to God's voice?

12. Explain the connection between sound, language, and

the restructuring of reality, as discussed in the section about "The Word of His Power."

13. How does speaking in tongues tap into the sound-based structure of reality?

14. Describe the concept of breaking patterns through speaking in tongues.

15. How does this act reshape reality and provide freedom from entrenched patterns?

16. Discuss the influence of sound on the physical and spiritual, as mentioned in the section about "The Influence of Sound on the Physical and Spiritual."

17. How do vibrations through the body's medium alter patterns within memories?

18. Synthesize the teachings from Luke 4 and John 4 in the context of Jesus' fasted state.

19. How does Jesus transform from a state of physical weakness to spiritual strength, and what role does the Holy Spirit play in this transformation?

20. Examine the distinction between the Spirit within and the Spirit upon a believer, as discussed by Kirby De Lanerolle. How does this distinction relate to empowerment, healing, and the transfer of spiritual power through physical actions?

21. Reflect on the idea of the Spirit upon someone and its connection to the laying-on of hands. Why does Kirby De Lanerolle caution against intentional laying on of hands, and how does the Spirit upon someone connect with their electromagnetic field?

CLOSING REFLECTIONS:

In concluding this exploration of the symbiotic relationship between science and spirituality through the lens of glossolalia, Kirby De Lanerolle's teachings offer a profound perspective on the mysteries of speaking in tongues. As we traverse the realms of interpretation, fasting, and the indwelling of the Holy Spirit, we find ourselves on a transformative journey toward a deeper understanding of our faith.

The interplay of sound, language, and spiritual power invites us to reconsider the ways in which we perceive and interact with the world around us. Through the lens of tongues, we discover not only a means of communication with the divine but a powerful tool for reshaping our reality, breaking free from entrenched patterns, and fostering a connection with the Spirit within and upon us.

.   .   .

As we reflect on De Lanerolle's teachings, we are challenged to embrace the mystical and the scientific, recognizing that the threads of spirituality are interwoven with the fabric of our existence. The call to fasting becomes a pathway to heightened spiritual sensitivity, a deliberate journey into the wilderness where the Spirit can lead and renew.

In the dynamic exchange between the Spirit within and upon us, we find a source of strength, healing, and empowerment. The caution against intentional laying-on of hands underscores the reverence for the divine flow, reminding us that spiritual power is not a commodity to be wielded but a force to be embraced with humility and authenticity.

Let this exploration serve as an invitation to delve deeper into the realms of faith, prayer, and spiritual experience. May the wisdom shared by Kirby De Lanerolle inspire contemplation, dialogue, and a renewed sense of awe for the mysteries that unfold at the intersection of science and Christianity. As we continue our individual journeys, may we carry with us the echoes of tongues spoken, the resonance of spiritual fasting, and the enduring truth that our connection with the divine is both intricate and infinite.

BONUS CHAPTER - PART TWO

INTRODUCTION:

The journey of faith is often marked by the pursuit of a deeper connection with the divine, a quest to tap into the profound mysteries that shape our spiritual existence. In this workbook, we explore a transformative aspect of prayer—speaking in tongues— and its profound implications for the believer's spiritual life. Drawing insights from biblical passages, personal experiences, and reflections on the intricate interplay between prayer, fasting, and the indwelling of the Holy Spirit, this workbook aims to guide readers through a thought-provoking exploration of the spiritual realm.

From the powerful encounters of Jesus in the wilderness to the Apostle Paul's teachings on the significance of praying in tongues, each section delves into the intricate layers of this spiritual practice. The author shares personal revelations, highlighting the role of speaking in tongues as a gateway to understanding God's will, interpreting divine messages, and fostering a deeper connection with the Spirit.

As you engage with the workbook, consider the questions posed at the end of each section. Reflect on your own experiences, draw parallels with the biblical narratives, and contemplate the implications of incorporating speaking in tongues into your prayer life. The journey to a more profound spiritual understanding is both personal and communal, and this workbook serves as a guide for those seeking to navigate the depths of prayer, tap into the spiritual gifts bestowed upon believers, and cultivate a richer connection with the divine.

WORKBOOK QUESTIONS:

1. Understanding the Prayer Experience:

Describe the author's experience when praying in tongues for an extended period.

According to the passage, why does the duration of prayer decrease after a significant session of praying in tongues?

2. The Shift in Luke 4:

What change does the author observe in Jesus after returning from the wilderness in Luke 4:14?

How does the author link fasting, speaking in tongues, and the Spirit coming upon a person based on Luke's experience?

3. Biblical Basis for Praying in Tongues:

Summarize the key points from 1 Corinthians 2 regarding the role of praying in tongues in deepening our connection with God.

How does the passage highlight the importance of praying in tongues for understanding God's plans?

4. The Truth About "Oneness":

What distinction does the author make between the New Age concept of "Oneness" and their own perspective?

Why does the author emphasize the importance of interpreting tongues as an inheritance?

5. Prophetic Experience:

Share the author's experience of interpreting tongues for urgent prayer.

What does this experience reveal about the difference between human understanding and God's guidance through interpreting tongues?

6. **Praying for the Unknown:**

How does the author approach praying for the unknown, especially when unsure of specific details?

Share a personal experience where your prayers took an unexpected direction, and the outcome surprised you.

7. **The Sabbath Gathering and Prophetic Words:**

According to Romans 8:26-28, how does the Spirit assist believers in their weaknesses?

How does the concept of synchronicity relate to speaking in tongues and preparing for prophetic words?

8. **The Power of Speaking in Tongues:**

Explain the author's analogy of receiving a promise and its activation in prayer.

How does speaking in tongues help in praying for someone's healing, according to the author?

9. **Understanding God's Will Through Tongues:**

Describe the significance of understanding God's will through speaking in tongues, as per the author.

Share a personal instance where speaking in tongues led to a better understanding of God's will in your life.

10. Conclusion and Tongue Interpreting Activation:

Summarize the main takeaway from the conclusion of the passage.

Try the Tongue Interpreting Activation and share your experience.

CLOSING REFLECTIONS:

In concluding this exploration of the spiritual dynamics surrounding speaking in tongues, may you find inspiration to embark on a captivating journey with God's Spirit. The interconnected threads of prayer, fasting, and the indwelling of the Holy Spirit, as illuminated through biblical narratives and personal anecdotes, unveil a pathway to a more profound spiritual experience.

As you navigate the questions and reflections within this workbook, may your understanding deepen, and may you encounter the transformative power that comes with speaking in tongues. Remember that this exploration merely scratches the surface of a vast and beautiful gift—one that is both attainable and profoundly impactful.

. . .

Let this workbook be a stepping stone into a world of spiritual exploration and revelation. As you pray, speak in tongues, and seek interpretation, may the Spirit within you overflow, and may you walk in the fullness of everything God has promised in His Word. May the journey ahead be filled with divine insights, transformative moments, and a heightened awareness of the Spirit's presence in your life. Embrace the gift of speaking in tongues, for in doing so, you open yourself to a deeper connection with the divine and an unfolding of God's plans for your journey of faith.

CONNECT WITH US

Follow this for hundreds of teachings, classes, and course from Tommy Miller and be sure the join the New Creation Collective group on Facebook!

Made in the USA
Middletown, DE
25 August 2024

59114346R00046